LEARNING ABOUT Animals

Catherine Veitch

The author would like to dedicate this book to her mother,
Jacqueline Veitch, who inspired her with a love of nature.

Raintree is an imprint of Capstone Global Library Limited, a company incorporated in England and Wales having its registered office at 7 Pilgrim Street, London, EC4V 6LB – Registered company number: 6695582

To contact Raintree:
Phone: 0845 6044371
Fax: + 44 (0) 1865 312263
Email: myorders@raintreepublishers.co.uk
Outside the UK please telephone +44 1865 312262.

Text © Capstone Global Library Limited 2014
First published in hardback in 2014
The moral rights of the proprietor have been asserted.

Edited by Dan Nunn, Rebecca Rissman, and Sian Smith
Designed by Joanna Hinton-Malivoire
Picture research by Mica Brancic
Production by Sophia Argyris
Originated by Capstone Global Library Ltd
Printed and bound in China by South China Printing Company Ltd

ISBN 978 1 406 26611 5
17 16 15 14 13
10 9 8 7 6 5 4 3 2 1

British Library Cataloguing in Publication Data
A catalogue record for this book is available from the British Library.

Acknowledgements
We would like to thank Michael Bright for his invaluable help in the preparation of this book.

We would also like to thank the following for permission to reproduce photographs: Alamy pp.18, 23 horn (© Avico Ltd); Getty Images p.21 inset (Oxford Scientific/David Cayless); Photoshot pp.16, 24 talon (© NHPA/Stephen Dalton); Shutterstock pp.4 (© Whytock), 5 inset (© PaulShlykov), 5 main (© REDSTARSTUDIO), 6 (© Cathy Keifer), 7 (© Sarel), 8 (© worldswildlifewonders), 9 (© Peter Krejzl), 10 (© Volodymyr Burdiak), 11 (© Irina Tischenko), 12 inset (© kool99), 12 main (© Dmitry Kalinovsky), 13 (© Herbert Kratky), 14 inset and main (© Sebastian Duda), 15 (© Eduard Kyslynskyy), 17 (© Christian Mueller), 19 (© Frantisek Czanner), 20 inset (© Mary Lane), 20 main (© Reinhold Leitner), 21main (© Mogens Trolle), 22 antler (© Peter Krejzl), 22 beak (© Volodymyr Burdiak), 22 crest (© Cathy Keifer), 22 fin, 23 gill (© Irina Tischenko), 23 hoof (© kool99), 23 mane (© Mogens Trolle), 23 scales (© worldswildlifewonders), 24 shell (© Reinhold Leitner), 24 snout, 24 spines (© Sebastian Duda).

Front cover photograph of a fallow deer reproduced with permission of Shutterstock (© Anthony Shaw Photography). Back cover photograph of a crab reproduced with permission of Shutterstock (© Sarel).

Every effort has been made to contact copyright holders of material reproduced in this book. Any omissions will be rectified in subsequent printings if notice is given to the publisher.

Contents

Anteater

nose

tail

Cat

claw

whiskers

Chameleon

crest

toes

Crab

eye

claw

Crocodile

snout

tooth

scales

Deer

antlers

ear

Fish

fin

gill

fin

Goat

horn

hoof

beard

Hare

ear

foot

13

Hedgehog

spines

snout

14

Mouse

paw

whiskers

15

Owl

wing

talon

Robin

beak

leg

Sheep

horn

woolly coat

Squirrel

tail

whiskers

19

Tortoise

claws

shell

mouth

Zebra

mane

hoof

Picture glossary

 **antlers** hard parts on an animal's head that look like branches. Animals can use antlers to fight or protect themselves.

 **beak** hard part of a bird's mouth. Beaks can be different shapes, and they are used to help birds eat.

 **crest** skin or feathers that stick up on top of an animal's head

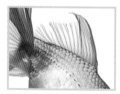 **fin** part of a fish that helps the fish to move through the water

 **gill** part of a fish that helps the fish to breathe

 **hoof** hard part of the foot of some animals. Horses and goats have hooves.

 **horn** hard, pointed part that grows out of an animal's head. Sheep and goats have horns.

 **mane** hair that grows on the necks of animals such as zebras, horses, or lions

 **scales** small, hard, overlapping parts that cover the skin of fish and reptiles

23

shell a hard body covering. Many animals with shells can hide inside them so that other animals cannot hurt them.

snout mouth and nose of some animals. A hedgehog has a snout.

spines stiff spikes. Spines can help to keep animals safe from other animals that want to eat them.

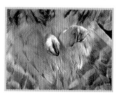

talon long, sharp, hooked claw on the foot of an eagle or another bird. Talons are used to catch and carry things.

Notes for parents and teachers

- Go on a trip to an animal park. Take this book along and ask the children to spot some of the animals shown in the book. Encourage the children to sketch or photograph what they see. Can they label the animals and animal parts?
- Use the images and labels to make a class book. Discuss the body parts of different animals and what the animals might use them for.